POWER UP!
LEARN ABOUT ENERGY

BY JULIA VOGEL

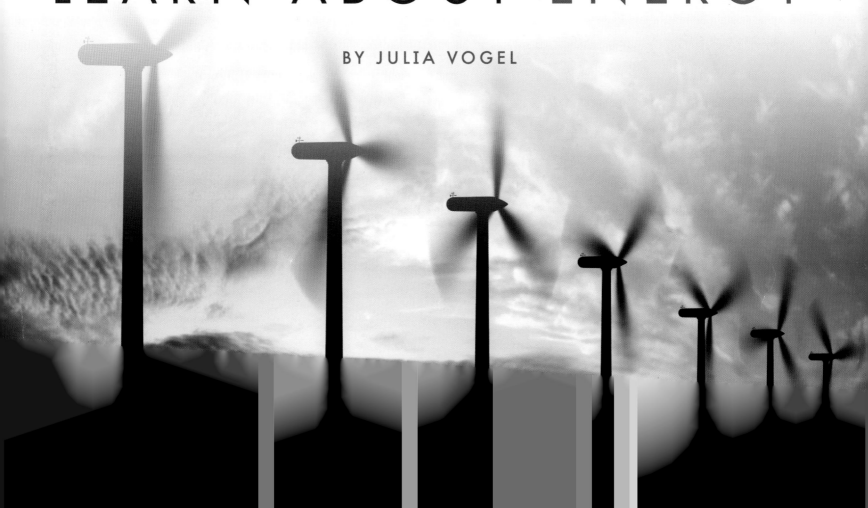

The Child's World®

Published by The Child's World®
1980 Lookout Drive • Mankato, MN 56003-1705
800-599-READ • www.childsworld.com

ACKNOWLEDGMENTS
The Child's World®: Mary Berendes, Publishing Director
Content Consultant: Paul Ohmann, PhD, Associate Professor of Physics,
    University of St. Thomas
The Design Lab: Design and production
Red Line Editorial: Editorial direction

PHOTO CREDITS: Stephen Strathdee/iStockphoto, cover, 1, 2, 3, 4, 6, 8, 10,
12, 14, 16, 18, 20, 22; Fotolia, 5 (top), 11 (top), 17, 18, 21 (top); Monkey
Business/Fotolia, 5 (bottom); Jan Schuler/Fotolia, 7; James Steidl/Fotolia, 9;
Brad Thompson/Fotolia, 11 (bottom); David Hughes/Fotolia, 13; Springfield
Gallery/Fotolia, 15 (top); Jaren Wicklund/Fotolia, 15 (bottom); Pei Lin/
Fotolia, 19; Robin Vinson/Fotolia, 21 (bottom); Jane Yamada, 23

LIBRARY OF CONGRESS CATALOGING-IN-PUBLICATION DATA
Vogel, Julia.
   Power up! Learn about energy / by Julia Vogel ; illustrated by Jane
Yamada.
     p. cm.
   ISBN 978-1-60253-512-1 (library bound : alk. paper)
   1. Power resources—Juvenile literature. I. Yamada, Jane. II. Title. III. Title:
Learn about energy.
   TJ163.23.V65 2010
   621.042—dc22   2010010980

Printed in the United States of America in Mankato, Minnesota.
July 2010
F11538

CONTENTS

Do It with Energy!

Run races with it.
Light your way with it.
Bake pizza with it.
Play drums with it.

Energy gets things going.
It makes things move or change.

Reading by
a flashlight
uses energy. ▶

Running
uses lots
of energy! ▶

4

All Kinds of Energy

There are many kinds of energy.

Fireworks shoot into the sky.
Their **motion** is a form of energy.
They explode into hot, bright flashes.
Heat and light are energy, too.

Bang! Boom!

Even sound is energy.

Watch the flash and hear the bang of energy from fireworks. ▶

6

It's easy to see that blasting fireworks have lots of energy. But fireworks on a shelf do, too. They have **potential energy**.

This kind of energy is stored. It can makes things happen later.

These fireworks have energy stored inside them. ▶

8

Energy can change from one kind to another.

An apple has stored food energy. Your body puts that energy to use. You use it to run and kick a ball.

The apple's energy has changed, but it did not go away.

Food gives your body energy. ▶

Kicking a soccer ball uses your body's energy. ▶

Starting with the Sun

Where did the apple's energy come from?

It came from the sun.

All green plants, including apple trees, use sunlight to grow. They store the sun's energy in their fruit, leaves, and stems.

Apple trees need energy from sunlight to grow. ▶

12

Then, animals eat the plants.
Energy moves into their bodies.

A glass of milk has energy from the sun.
When you drink the milk,
you get that energy!

Cows eat grass
to get energy. ▶

Energy comes
from the sun,
through the
cow, into the
milk, and into
your body. ▶

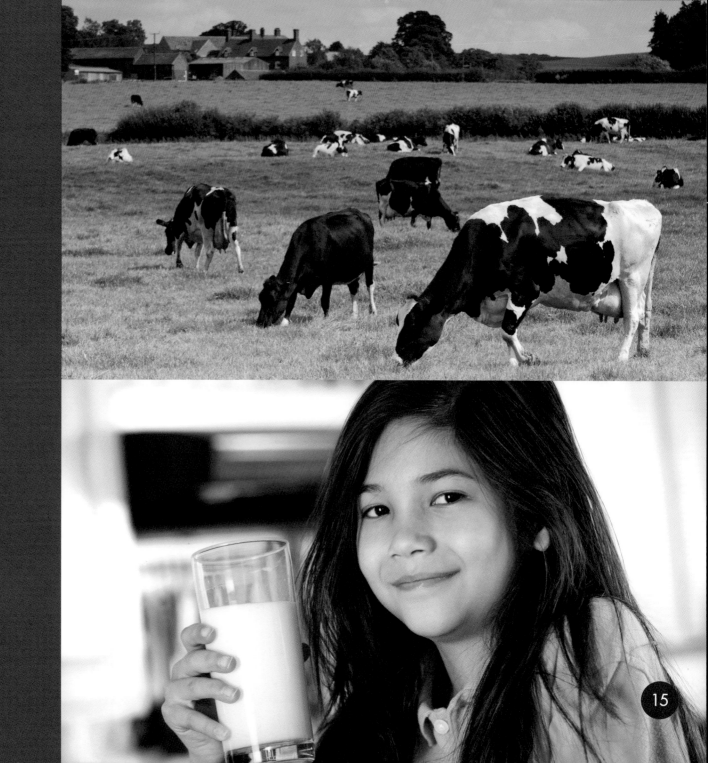

Energy in Fuel

Even the **fuels** that power our cars and factories store energy from the sun.
Oil, coal, and natural gas are called **fossil fuels**. They are the remains of plants and animals that lived millions of years ago. Those living things once got energy from the sun.

But fossil fuels can cause problems.
They **pollute** the air.
And someday they will run out.

Using some fuels causes pollution. ▶

16

Scientists are looking for better ways to power cars and factories.

Sunlight, wind, and ocean tides could replace fossil fuels someday. These energy sources do not pollute. They will not run out.

Ocean waves have energy. ▶

Solar panels turn sunlight into energy we can use. ◀

Getting the Job Done

Think of all the energy used during your day.

It takes energy to run your school bus and to heat your home.

It takes energy to make the electricity that powers your computer.

Your school bus needs energy to run. ▶

You use energy every time you turn on your computer. ▶

Your body uses energy
    to move,
    grow,
    breathe,
    and even sleep.

You are even using energy
to read this book!

Ways to Save Energy

Burning fossil fuels harms the planet. Here are some ways you can cut back on using them.

WHAT TO DO	HOW IT HELPS
Keep your house cooler in winter.	This cuts back on oil or natural gas, as most houses are heated using those fossil fuels.
Turn off lights, TVs, and computers when you're not using them.	This saves electricity. Most electricity in the United States comes from burning coal at power plants.
Don't waste food.	This saves on fossil fuels used to grow food and bring it to the supermarket.
Take the bus instead of driving places in cars.	This reduces use of gasoline, which comes from oil.

Words to Know

fossil fuels (FOS-ul FYOOLZ): Fossil fuels can be oil, coal, or natural gas. Fossil fuels come from plants and animals that lived millions of years ago.

fuels (FYOOLZ): Fuel are things that store energy. Food is fuel for your body.

motion (MOH-shun): Motion is another word for moving. Motion is a form of energy.

pollute (puh-LOOT): To pollute is to make things dirty in a way that harms Earth. Burning fossil fuels pollutes the air.

potential energy (poh-TEN-shul EN-er-jee): Potential energy is stored energy that can be used later. An apple has potential energy that is put to use by your body.